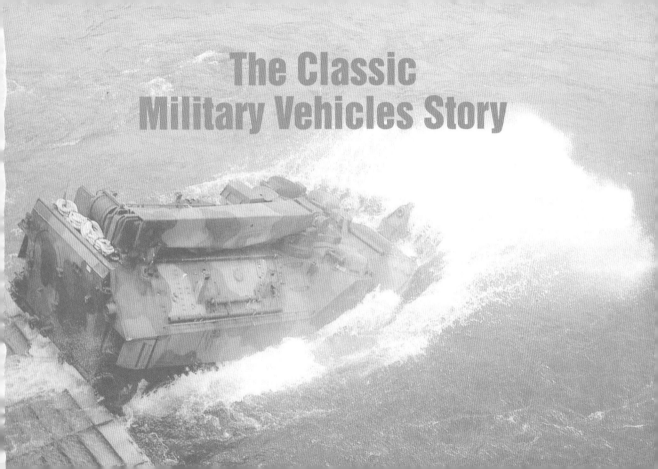

The Classic
Military Vehicles Story

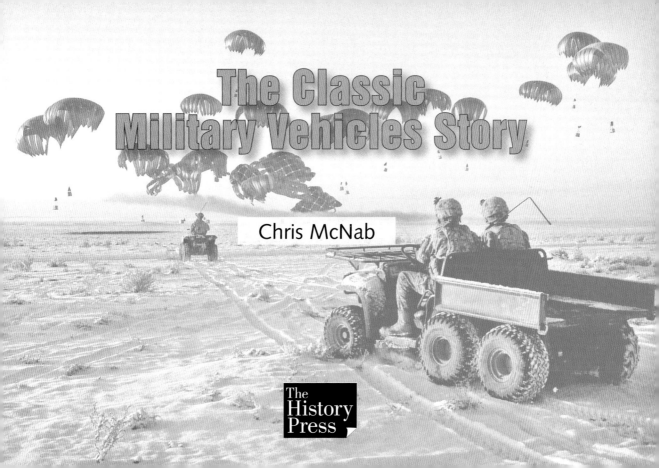

The Classic Military Vehicles Story

Chris McNab

The History Press

Published in the United Kingdom in 2011 by
The History Press
The Mill · Brimscombe Port · Stroud · Gloucestershire · GL5 2QG

British Library Cataloguing in Publication Data
A catalogue record for this book is available from the British
Library.

ISBN 978-0-7524-6204-2

Cover images: *Front*: A British Chieftain tank. *Back*: A Willys
'Jeep' armed with three Vickers K machine guns. (both images
courtesy of Cody Images).

Typesetting and origination by The History Press
Printed in China

CONTENTS

ACKNOWLEDGEMENTS

There are several people I would like to thank for their assistance in producing this book. As always, I much appreciate the friendship and support of Jo de Vries at The History Press, and to all the design and editorial team there. Special thanks go to Ted Nevill of Cody Images, who always manages to produce an excellent selection of photographs under short timescales.

The roots of the internal-combustion engine go back deep into history. Elements of what would become the world's principal motive power are detected as far back as the 13th century, at least in concept. Yet in practical terms it was really the second half of the 19th century in which the internal-combustion engine became both an efficient design and a production reality. During the 1860s, engineers such as the Belgian Jean Joseph Etienne Lenoir, Frenchman Alphonse Beau de Rochas and Germans Nikolaus Otto (helped by the future famous names Gottlieb Daimler and Wilhlem Maybach) and Karl Benz, amongst others, made the internal-combustion engine a practical alternative to steam power.

Furthermore, on 29 January 1886, Karl Benz patented the first petrol-powered automobile, propelled by a four-stroke engine. By 1888 the Benz Motorwagen was in production, and a revolution in personal and eventually commercial transport took place.

◄ A de Dion-Bouton motorcycle, here converted rather implausibly into a military vehicle by bolting a Maxim machine gun to the front. The conversion was made in 1899 by the man pictured here, one F.R. Simms. (Cody Images)

7

Despite the German lead, mass production of automobiles, based on line assembly technologies, was actually an American invention, pioneered by the Oldsmobile Company in 1902. Henry Ford later famously refined the principle, the great Model T vehicle rolling off his assembly lines at a rate of several every hour. Once such volume production was copied abroad, the world was on its way to a transport revolution.

The internal-combustion engine … is ready to carry whatever one wants, wherever it is needed, at all speeds and distances.

General Charles de Gaulle

Often in the history of engineering, developments in the civilian world inspire the military community, and the advent of the automobile is a case in point. At the end of the 19th century, military technology was also undergoing huge changes. The invention of breech-loading machine guns, rifles and artillery had exponentially transformed the volume of firepower a modern army could generate. Increased firepower meant increased ammunition consumption, which in turn demanded more efficient, scalable logistics. Railways – another transport revolution in that most innovative of centuries – could take ammunition and troops so far, but alternative means were required to shift them from the railhead to the battlefront. Steam-powered tractors and trucks had both entered service by the end of the

9

The internal combustion engine was more practical for military purposes than steam power, as it delivered instant power from a convenient fuel source. Here US soldiers mount trucks during the Mexican expedition in 1916. (Cody Images)

Soldiers gather around a mighty steam engine in the early years of the twentieth century. Such vehicles delivered formidable traction, but little in the way of speed. (Cody Images)

1860s, but by the early 1900s petrol- and diesel-powered vehicles were starting to take over and expand possibilities. Although for many decades to come most soldiers' equipment would still be drawn towards battle by horses, this new breed of vehicle offered exciting new options for improving the flow of war materiel. To this day, logistics remains the primary function of the bulk of the world's military vehicles.

As we shall see, internal-combustion powered vehicles provided the possibility of a whole new breed of mobile weapons systems. It was a relatively natural step to marry firepower with vehicle, and once embraced by the military, the automobile revolution met a whole world of tactical and utility requirements, in turn producing staff cars, tanks, armoured cars, artillery tractors, transporters, communications vehicles, ambulances, armoured personnel carriers, amphibious assault vehicles, mine-clearers and numerous other types. As such vehicles proliferated, the battlefield was utterly reshaped in terms of speed of manoeuvre and the firepower deployed, and mechanization became central to victory.

This book will describe a journey through the landmarks of military vehicle design since the beginning of the twentieth century to the present day. The technological evolution within that time period is astonishing, stretching from vehicles that offered walking-pace maximum speeds and the firepower of a rifle, up to modern combat vehicles capable of high speeds on both land and water and the capabilities to destroy entire city blocks in a few seconds. In telling this story, however, we will also acknowledge the human truth that no matter how powerful the vehicle, there is always a human being inside whose survival depends upon it.

In 1899, a photograph was taken of a potentially new generation of fighting vehicle. It consisted of a de Dion-Bouton four-wheel motorcycle, looking like a cross between a pram and a car and powered by a diminutive rear-mounted petrol engine, but with a Maxim machine gun bolted to a front bracket by one F.R. Simms (see Introduction – the rider in the photograph on p.7). The machine gun was to be operated by the driver, who in the photograph decorously steers the vehicle one handed while aiming the weapon. A modicum of armoured protection for the rider came from a shield mounted around the gun.

To modern eyes, the de Dion-Bouton fighting vehicle appears almost laughable. Yet it is an important innovation, not least because it represents the concept of combining weapons and vehicles, providing a mobile platform with greater firepower than a horse-mounted cavalryman, and without all the logistical hassles of producing bulky fodder for a hungry animal. Others were more ambitious, however. They saw the potential for creating *armoured* vehicles, machines that not only projected firepower, but at the same time protected the crew inside from return fire.

◄ *This German Ehrhardt BAK 1906 armoured car is little more than a truck covered with armour plate and surmounted with a turret holding a 50mm cannon. Such were typical designs of the early twentieth century. (Cody Images)*

➤ *The British Whippet light tank/armoured car was designed as a faster, more mobile complement to the slower heavy tanks. It was armed with four machine guns and had a top speed of 13.4km/h (8.3mph). (Cody Images)*

Did you know?
Many early armoured vehicles were armoured in name only – the metal on the 1904 Austro-Daimler armoured car, for example, was a mere 4mm thick, scarcely enough to stop a common rifle bullet.

What we see from the 1890s, therefore, was the emergence of what we today call the armoured car. Military designers took the chassis of civilian or sporting vehicles and built upon them armoured superstructures, complete with weapons

16

◀◀◀ The US also produced several varieties of armoured car during the World War I years. Here is an Armoured Car No. 2, dated to around 1916. (Cody Images)

◀ The French Renault FT 17 was a particularly important French light tank/armoured car, as it introduced the fully rotating gun turret, hence providing the vehicle with a 360-degree fire capability. (Cody Images)

Did you know?

The maximum road speed of most early armoured cars was in the region of 45km/h (28mph), although on larger vehicles that speed dropped as low as 20km/h (13mph).

(typically machine guns) projecting through ports or mounted in turrets. In 1900, the British John Fowler & Company clad a steam traction engine in armour plate and used it for battlefield logistics during the Boer War in 1901–02. Furthermore, in 1904 the Austrian engineer Paul Daimler took a standard car chassis and surrounded the passenger compartment with thin armour plate, topping off the whole superstructure with a rear-positioned revolving turret fitted with a single Maxim machine gun or two Schwarzlose machine guns. It was manned by a crew of four, and its 30kW (4hp) 4-cylinder engine could power it to a maximum road speed of 45km/h (28mph). Auguring the future of military vehicles, the 'Austro-Daimler' also had four-wheel drive, giving it a decent off-road capability. Two years later and the French produced a similar vehicle in the form of the Charron, Giradot & Voigt (CGV) 1906. This was constructed along similar lines to the Daimler armoured car, but its turret was armed with a single French 8mm machine gun.

By the time World War I broke out in 1914, armoured cars had become part of the arsenal of most European nations, being produced by the likes of Schneider (France), Vickers (Britain) and Ehrhardt (Germany). The latter, in 1906, manufactured an armoured car that even incorporated an upward-firing 'anti-balloon canon', creating the world's first mobile anti-aircraft vehicle. Many of these armoured cars were intended for light scouting duties in colonial outposts. Typically, they were heavy and slow, and did not cope well with the particularly difficult terrain.

The limitations of early armoured cars were revealed during the global conflict that erupted in 1914. While useful on roads, they were simply unable to cope with the mud and tortured landscape into which many fronts descended. (They still found applications in flat, mud-free environments, such as the Middle East.) The true significance of the conflict for wheeled vehicles was in logistics. Horse-drawn supply columns still dominated, but armies increasingly turned to the power of diesel and petrol to transport ammunition, equipment and supplies to depots near the frontlines. Many of the vehicles used were simply requisitioned civilian types. Germany, for example, appropriated or put into reserve 3,000 tractors, 7,700 heavy trucks and 50,000 cars. At a more ad hoc level, the British also used adapted London buses as crude troop transporters.

▲ *A column of British trucks rolls towards the frontline. The truck at the front appears to be the Leyland Three-Tonner, thousands of which were used in the war by the British Army and Royal Flying Corps. (Cody Images)*

➤ A convoy of Ford Model T pick-up trucks, in British service, moves through African landscape in 1917. Ford vehicles were used in a range of military roles in World War I, from haulage through to field ambulances. (Cody Images)

Did you know?
At the battle of the Marne in September 1914, the French ordered 600 Parisian taxi drivers to deliver 6000 troops to the battlefront.

By far the greatest producer of trucks used for military purposes during the conflict was the United States. The Packard 3-ton Army Truck – originally intended as a gun tractor but repurposed as a troop and supplies carrier – was actually in service before the war began, and it served throughout the conflict. The official wartime government-produced trucks, built according to specifications from the Quartermaster Corps, were known as 'Liberty trucks', and came in 1.5-ton (Class A) or 3–5-ton (Class B) versions, entering service in 1917. Other US manufacturers such as White, GMC and

Requisitioned civilian types made up a large part of the military vehicles on the Western Front. The London double-decker bus here has been repurposed to deploy carrier pigeons. (Cody Images)

‚Little Willie', the forerunner of the British Mk I tank, was powered by a 78kW (105hp) Daimler engine, and its outer shell was actually boiler plate rather than armour. (Cody Images)

During World War I, trucks were soon applied to combat roles as well as logistical tasks. Here what appear to be Thorneycroft trucks are mounted with 13pdr 9cwt anti-aircraft guns. (Cody Images)

Did you know?
Such was the success of the Nash Quad that it led to Nash becoming the world's largest producer of military trucks by the end of the war.

Nash Motors delivered more than 60,000 vehicles for military use, including the Nash Quad, which offered the four-wheel drive capability so useful over the terrain of the Western Front. US trucks were also sold in large numbers to the Allies. Britain, for example, made heavy use of the Ford T cargo truck, adapting it for various utility purposes, including serving as ambulances.

ENTER THE TANK

While trucks and cars became a vital part of behind-the-lines support, on the battlefield itself an armoured vehicle was about to emerge that would change the very nature of land warfare. This vehicle, what we today call the 'tank', would not have been possible without an alternative form of traction to the standard wheel, which delivered a high ground pressure and was therefore unsuitable for use over soft ground. The answer was the 'continuous track', more popularly known as the 'caterpillar track'. Instead of wheels, this system utilized a continuous band of metal links that wrapped around drive wheels. It offered several appreciable advantages, including a low ground pressure, the confidence to negotiate soft terrain and the equal ability to cross trenches. Early experiments with this form of drive dated back to the 1830s, but during the early 1900s the system had been developed to

25

A British Mk I tank during trials in 1916. Here we can clearly see one of the 6pdr guns mounted in a sponson on the side. The definitive Mk IV version used shorter-barrelled guns. (Cody Images)

a production state by various commercial manufacturers, for applications in industries such as farming and logging. What British military engineers spotted was a way to utilize the continuous track for an entirely different form of armoured vehicle.

In 1915, the Admiralty Landships Committee was formed under the authority of the First Lord of the Admiralty, Winston Churchill, with the purpose of creating a powerfully armed, well-armoured fighting machine to break the deadlock on the Western Front. The first convincing prototype was 'Little Willie', essentially a three-crew armoured box powered by a Daimler 6-cylinder petrol engine to a monotonous top speed of 3.2km/h (2mph). It utilized the continuous-track drive, but was steered mainly by two external wheels connected at the rear. The design was

Did you know?

The crews of early tanks often worn metal-link chain masks over their faces, to protect themselves from the splinters of metal flying off the interior of the vehicle from bullet impacts outside.

modified to produce 'Big Willie' in late 1915, which had an improved trench-crossing capability, and it was this model that led to the first production tank in history, the Mk I, of which the British Army ordered 100 in February 1916.

The Mk I was revolutionary. Rhomboidal in shape, with its continuous track running around its outer edges, it had an eight-man crew (four of whom were gunners) and a top speed of 6.4km/h (4mph).

Its outer armour had a maximum depth of 12mm (0.47in.), sufficient to stop most contemporary small-arms fire, although insufficient to withstand a hit from an artillery shell. In its 'Male' version it was armed with two 6pdr cannon mounted in side sponsons and four Hotchkiss machine guns; the 'Female' infantry support version had six machine guns only.

The Mk I tank was infernal to operate, filled with deafening noise and choking gun and exhaust fumes, and it was plagued by mechanical unreliability. Subsequent versions, including the major production model, the Mk IV of 1917, improved the situation progressively, although they remained difficult vehicles to man. But there was no denying their impact on the battlefield, at least in terms of shock value. First used during the battle of the Somme in 1916, and prominently at the battle of Cambrai the following year, the tanks could grind through barbed wire that was impenetrable to infantry, blazing away at close range with cannon and machine gun. The crew remained inside, shielded from the bullets flying around them. Although the early tanks were not battle winning – at least, not yet – they proved that heavily armed, armoured vehicles could have a significant place in fighting wars.

I managed to get astride one of the German trenches... There were some Germans in the dug-outs and I shall never forget the look on their faces.

Captain H.W. Mortimore, who commanded one of the first tanks ever to go into battle, 15 September 1916

◄ *The cumbersome French St Charmond tank was an awkward design, the nose of which tended to dig into the ground when the tank was travelling across uneven ground. Here we can see the main armament, a 75mm gun. (Cody Images)*

Britain was not the only one to be developing tanks, however. The French were also pushing ahead with their own designs at the same time; in fact, France would produce more tanks (3,870) during the war than Britain (2,693). The first (1917) was the Schneider CA-1, weighing 14.8 tonnes (14.6 long tons), manned by a crew of seven men and armed with a single 75mm gun plus two machine guns. In action, the CA-1 and its improved versions gave a generally poor performance, its fuel tanks being easy to catch fire and struggling manfully when crossing wide trenches or shell-holes. An alternative vehicle that also entered service in 1917 was the St Charmond, unusual for the large portions of hull that overhung the tracks at the front and rear. It again was armed with a single 75mm main gun and multiple (four) machine guns, and just like the Schneider it also waded awkwardly across rough ground.

Yet we must not over-emphasize the failings of these vehicles. These were early days for armoured firepower, and the concept proved itself sufficiently for tanks to enter service with most combatants. The Germans developed the large and unwieldy Sturmpanzerwagen A7V, essentially a chronically unstable iron room armed with a 57mm gun and six machine guns,

Did you know?

The Holt Company also produced a steam-powered tank, which had the unfortunate tendency of turning into a cauldron if a bullet punctured one of the boilers.

The Schneider Char d'Assaut (CA) tank was another French wartime tank design. It was armed with a 75mm cannon and two Hotchkiss 8mm machine guns, and was manned by a crew of six. (Cody Images)

➤ World War I saw motorized logistics used on an extensive scale for the first time. Here we see a group of despatch rides, on Douglas motorbikes, in front of a varied collection of militarized trucks. (Cody Images)

British soldiers have here converted a simple flatbed truck into a mobile weapons platform by adding a Vickers 0.303in. machine gun. Such designs would have been more suited to security duties than trench warfare. (Cody Images)

with a road speed of 12.9km/h (8mph) – only about twenty were produced. From America came the Holt Gas-Electric tank, which utilized a Holt petrol engine to power a generator, supplying electricity to drive motors. The types of tank also diversified. French and British designers produced the first light tanks, smaller and lighter armoured vehicles with improved cross-country and on-road performance. They included the British Medium Tank A 'Whippet' and the French Renault FT-17; the former could do a positively giddy 13.4km/h (8.3mph) on a good surface.

By the end of World War I, therefore, the world's armies had several new war-fighting and utility vehicle types in their arsenal. They included heavy tanks, light tanks, armoured cars, trucks and various logistical vehicles, such as artillery tractors (many of these hefty monsters remained steam-powered). The interwar period would see both vehicles and tactical concepts refined, laying the foundations for the centrality of armour and mechanization in the next world war.

The interwar period reshaped the nature of military vehicles, both tactically and technologically. Britain, France, Germany, the Soviet Union and Italy all began to draw up more ornate doctrines of mechanized and armoured warfare, looking at ways in which new generations of faster, more powerful vehicles could speed up manoeuvre, achieve decisive breakthroughs and support the infantry on the attack.

In the world of tanks, three classes of armoured vehicle emerged: heavy, medium and light. Heavy tanks were designed to smash through enemy defences, and included types such as the French Char 2C and the Soviet T-35 Model 1932. Both of

Near Moscow in 1939, a large body of T-26 tanks conduct manoeuvres. The T-26 was a light infantry support tank, and it was the most numerous vehicle in Soviet armoured service at the time of the German invasion in 1941. (Cody Images)

▶ The M1 Combat Car was a light armoured vehicle used by US cavalry forces from the late 1930s until 1943, by which time it was obsolete. Less than a hundred of all variants were produced. (Cody Images)

these tanks were multi-turret designs; the T-35 Model 32, for example, had one main turret mounting a 76mm howitzer, plus four sub-turrets, each armed with either a cannon or a machine gun. Although the multi-turret approach would persist in some designs into World War II, it was generally dropped across all classes of tank in favour of the single turret, armed with a convincing cannon able to take on both enemy fortifications and opposing tanks.

A step below the heavy tank class was the medium tank. In neat theory, the medium tank was designed to exploit the gaps created by its heavier brethren, using its speed and firepower to push behind the frontlines. Examples of the type include the Vickers Medium Mk II, armed with a quick-firing (QF) 3pdr gun and with a top speed of 21km/h (15mph). Rather more impressive on the speed stakes was the American Christie series of tanks. Despite weighing nearly the same as the Vickers tank, the T3E2 could gallop along off-road at up to 32km/h (20mph), powered by a V12 Curtiss engine. The Soviets went even further, applying the Christie suspension system (which had independent suspension for each wheel) in their BT-2 fast tank – with a maximum speed of 100km/h (62mph), the name was apt.

… the internal combustion engine which, if it is armoured, possesses such a fire power and shock power that the rhythm of battle corresponds to that of its movements.

General Charles de Gaulle

Did you know?
The Soviet T-35 1932 tank was powered by a M-17M 12-cylinder petrol engine that generated 373kW (500hp) and a max speed of 30km/h (18.6mph).

Then came the light tanks category, which sat just above armoured cars. In essence, light tanks served a similar purpose to armoured cars, replacing the traditional mounted cavalry in reconnaissance and fast assault roles. Typically mounted with machine guns or very light cannon, classic examples of the light tank include the Vickers T15 and Matilda, the Italian Fiat 3000 Model 1930 and the Soviet T-26 Model 1933.

The general principle behind the heavy, medium and light classifications was that the heavier vehicles were slower but had more substantial armour and armament, while the lighter vehicles had more insubstantial armour and armament, but the advantages that came with speed. During the 1930s, however, there was a gradual shift in priorities, incom-plete by the beginning of World War II in 1939.

Generally speaking, and with much variation between nations, tanks began to acquire greater depth of armour and more powerful guns, essential qualities if they were to survive against both enemy tanks and the new breeds of anti-tank weapons entering service. The German *Wehrmacht*, finally freed from its Versailles Treaty shackles in 1935, embraced this evolution better than most, and entered World War II with one of the most powerful and tactically proficient armoured forces in Europe. The two key German tanks of the 1930s were the PzKpfw II and PzKpfw III. The former emerged in 1934, and was mainly armed with machine guns only (at least during the interwar years), and had an armour depth of 13mm (0.51in.) in

◁ A large group of Soviet BT-7 tanks rolls forward during pre-war manoeuvres. The BT-7 was lightly armed and armoured, but could do a top speed of 86km/h (53mph). (Cody Images)

◀◀◀ Vast formations of PzKpfw Is parade before Nazi dignitaries at Nuremberg in the late 1930s. The display looks impressive, but the Panzer I was virtually outdated by the end of the Poland campaign in September 1939. (Cody Images)

◀ The Spanish Civil War (1936–39) provided the Germans with a testing ground for their concepts of armoured and mechanized warfare. Here we see German motorbike and sidecar combinations leading an SdKfz 265 command tank and a PzKpfw I light tank. (Cody Images)

the Ausf B variant. Between its entering service and the production of the final variant (Ausf F) in 1942, the armour crept up to 80mm (3.1in.) thick. The PzKpfw III medium tank more than doubled its armour depth between 1936, its in-service date, and 1938, and its firepower went from a 37mm gun to a longer-range 50mm gun by 1939. Just before the outbreak of the war, the PzKpfw IV entered service with a 75mm gun – variants of this vehicle would become the core of the German Panzer force.

The German armoured force set a benchmark against which other armies could be measured. Some emerge from the comparison favourably. The Soviets, for example, upgraded many of their medium tanks from 37mm or 47mm guns up to the 75mm standard during the 1930s, and created one of the greatest tanks of the war in doing so – the T-34 (see next chapter). The French had a robust force of more than 2,600 tanks in 1939, including the Char Léger FCM-36 and the advanced Somua S-35, which had a cast rather than riveted hull and an armour depth of up to 55mm (2.2in.). Yet only the Char B heavy tank had a 75mm gun, and only 172 of those were produced by 1939. British, Italian, US and Japanese armoured forces were even more heavily dominated by light and medium machine-gun armed types. The scene was set for many unequal struggles.

MULTIPLE TYPES

The interwar period was not only fruitful for developments in tank technology. Indeed, the 1920s and 1930s were also

The tank marks as great a revolution in land warfare as an armoured steamship would have marked had it appeared amongst the toilsome triremes of Actium.

General Sir Ian Hamilton

The Japanese Type 93 Sumida armoured car could be converted from road travel to travel on rails in a matter of about 10 minutes. It was a hefty vehicle used primarily in the Sino-Japanese War (1937–45). (Cody Images)

Did you know?

The PzKpfw IV was the most prolific battle tank in the German armoured inventory – 9,000 were produced between 1939 and 1945.

This diminutive vehicle is a Polish TKS tankette, a two-man armoured car fitted with a single 7.92mm Hotchkiss wz.25 machine gun. These were no match for German armour in 1939. (Cody Images)

notable for increasing the sheer variety of what we classify as military vehicles. For utility vehicles such as trucks and staff cars, the progressive armies abandoned the old policy of using civilian types and oversaw the construction of dedicated military vehicles suited to operating robustly in rough conditions. The Soviets thereby created a range of trucks that would see them through the war and into the Cold War period, vehicles such as the GAZ-AA 4x2 1.5-ton truck, a licence-built copy of the Ford AA Model 1929, and the ZiS-5, which remained in production between 1931 and 1958. The Germans produced a similarly excellent vehicle in the Henschel 33D1, which had a maximum road speed of 60km/h (37mph), and in Britain the likes of Morris-Commercial, Leyland, AEC and Bedford worked up a range of serviceable trucks for needs ranging from light utility to heavy haulage.

△ Although the Belgian company Fabrique Nationale would later become famous for making small-arms, here we see another of their early products – motorbikes for Belgian Army despatch riders. (Cody Images)

Specialist vehicles also proliferated during the interwar years. As the models and sizes of artillery pieces increased, artillery tractors became more critical to the mechanization of armies. A classic example was the British AEC Matador 0853, a 4x4 wheeled medium artillery tractor powered by a 70.8kW (95hp) AEC 6-cylinder engine;

it was generally used for drawing the QF
3.75in. AA gun and the 5.5in. Medium
Gun. Wheeled propulsion had its limitations
over rough ground, though, so tracked and

semi-tracked designs were also developed
and fielded. Semi-tracked versions included
the German Sdkfz 7 and 9 and the French
P 107. The Japanese and Russians, by

contrast, preferred fully tracked artillery tractors, often influenced by agricultural designs but with a military twist in fittings and equipment.

It should be noted that the half-track design proved particularly amenable for the development of what are known today as armoured personnel carriers (APCs), vehicles designed to deploy small squads of infantry safely to the combat zone, and deliver additional firepower when they got there. The awkward-looking British Burford-Kegresse half-track had a drive track made of metal-reinforced rubber, but it could carry up to twelve infantrymen plus its two-man crew at a pace of 35km/h (22mph). It was armed with one or two 0.303in. Vickers machine guns.

The French adopted a more innovative approach to troop carriage in the Lorraine 38L. It consisted of a fully tracked tractor, which could carry six passengers, plus

▼ *Armoured vehicles soon proved that they had many applications other than war-fighting. This Soviet light tank has been converted into a simple bridgelaying vehicle. (Cody Images)*

▶ *The French Laffly W15T was an all-terrain vehicle based on the early S15 artillery tractor model. When it wasn't towing a gun, it could be used as a personnel carrier or reconnaissance vehicle. (Cody Images)*

▶▶ *Experiments in amphibious tanks began prior to World War II. Here is a Soviet T-37 tank, the first fully amphibious tank to enter mass production and military service. (Cody Images)*

a towed covered trailer that held an additional six soldiers. The true pioneers of early APCs, however, were the Germans. In 1939, the 1st Panzer Division received the SdKfz 251 half-track, capable of holding up to twelve personnel and transporting them at a speed of 52.5km/h (32.5mph), with support fire from two 7.62mm MG34 machine guns. What would prove to be so impressive about this half-track, and similar versions developed during the war years, was its versatility as a platform. In total, no fewer than twenty-two special-purpose variants were produced during the vehicle's lifetime, these including communications vehicles, ambulances and rocket launchers.

Looking back to the beginning of the interwar period, the 1920s brought the introduction of history's first practical self-propelled gun, the British Birch Gun, in 1925. Mounting artillery upon a vehicle chassis was attractive to tacticians on many levels, not least because it offered the prospect of engaging the enemy but then quickly moving before return fire could be brought to bear. The Birch Gun took the chassis of a Vickers medium tank and mounted it with an 18pdr field gun. The Mk II version followed shortly after, which swapped the 18pdr for a 75mm field gun,

Did you know?

Between 1936 and 1939, the Soviets built 42,000 GAZ-A staff cars, which were essentially licence-built copies of the American 1927 Ford Model A.

the new gun permitting the elevation range necessary for it to engage both ground and aerial targets. Few Birch Guns were built, and there was little interest in integrating them substantially into the British Army, so they were pulled from service in 1931. It would take wartime conditions for the British to revisit the self-propelled gun concept.

The list of specialist vehicles produced between 1918 and 1939 is a substantial one. It includes mobile workshops, ambulance vehicles, tank transporters, communications vehicles and bridging trucks. Yet while the technologies of military vehicles were developing rapidly, many authorities were still uncertain about the applications of armour and mechanization in modern warfare. The Germans, at least in practical implementation, were probably the most advanced in theory and training, and the events of 1939 and 1940 would dispel all illusions about the centrality of vehicle power on the battlefield.

The opening German campaigns of the war, in Poland in 1939 and Western and Northern Europe in 1940, were defined by what mainly post-war historians labelled *Blitzkrieg* ('Lightning War'). At its core, this group of tactical principles is based around focused, fast penetrations by armoured units through weak points in the enemy frontline, the tanks punching deep into the enemy rear areas to encircle army formations, destroy communications and unsettle the tactical response. Following the breakthrough were mechanized and traditional foot-slogging infantry, who would consolidate the gains.

The first two years of the war seem to be the ultimate vindication of *Blitzkrieg*, as previously mighty opponents of Germany fell in a matter of weeks. Panzer forces used specialist command-and-control vehicles such as the Panzerbefehlswagen III Ausf E to coordinate the tanks and other units on the battlefield. (This tank actually had a dummy gun fitted on the turret, to avoid drawing the enemy's attention to the vehicle's command role.) Using superior powers of movement, the German Panzer IIIs and IVs inflicted very heavy losses on Allied light and medium tanks, although at the same time learnt that the light PzKpfw Is and IIs were too insubstantial to take a place in the vanguard. In North Africa in 1940 and 1941, the Germans also took a brutal toll of British/Commonwealth Matilda, Valentine and Stuart tanks, not least because the Panzer forces operated in close cooperation with anti-tank guns.

In June 1941, Hitler widened his imperial ambitions when he invaded the Soviet Union in Operation Barbarossa. Although

◀ Japan's tanks were generally poor-quality types with little in the way of decent armour or armament. The Type 89A Chi-Ro tank seen here had a maximum armour depth of just 17mm (0.66in.). (Cody Images)

A PzKpfw IV tank, here seen painted white for snow camouflage during operations in the Ukraine. The Panzer IV was the workhorse tank of the German Army, and its chassis was used for a variety of other vehicles, including tank-destroyers and the Wirlbewind anti-aircraft vehicle. (Cody Images)

the first months of the German campaign cut swathes of destruction through Soviet forces, and was brought to a stop only before gates of Moscow in December 1941, for the Panzer arm there was also a shock in the form of one of the greatest tanks in history – the T-34.

DEFINING TANKS

The T-34 had entered production in 1940. Riding on the Christie suspension system and particularly wide tracks, it delivered very low ground pressure, ideal for traversing the snows and mud of Russia's seasonal extremes, and at speeds of up to 53km/h (33mph) – faster than both the Panzer III and IV. It had thick armour (up to 80mm/3.1in.), the presented depth of which was increased by the hull and turret having steeply sloped sides to deflect enemy shot. Most importantly, it was armed as standard with a decent 75mm gun.

In short, the T-34 was fast, powerful and well-armoured. Many German tank crews watched in dismay as their shot bounced off the T-34's steel, or they were outmanoeuvred and outgunned in action. Furthermore, in 1943 the Soviets began producing an even more formidable variant, the T-34/85, which had an 85mm gun and thicker armour around the turret and hull. Only the poor state of training among Soviet tank crews prevented the T-34 from

Did you know?
The tracks on the
T-34/76 were 475mm
(18.7in.) wide.
The tracks on the
early Panzer IVs, by
contrast, were just
360mm (14.2in.) wide.

➤ *The British tank here is the Matilda, which served the Allies well in reconnaissance roles during the campaigns in North Africa, and also in some Pacific campaigns. Its principal armament was a 2pdr cannon. (Cody Images)*

◀ The US M3 Lee/Grant tank served in both the American and British armies and featured a dual turret design: the hull-mounted side turret held a 75mm gun, while the top turret had a 37mm gun. The high profile unfortunately made the tank easy to target. (Cody Images)

having a crushing effect on German forces. To make matters worse for the Axis, the T-34 was quick to produce, and including post-war manufacture more than 84,000 rolled out of Soviet factories.

Germany's answer to the T-34, and other high-volume Allied tanks such as the US Sherman, came in the form of improved versions of the PzKpfw IV and also some of the most impressive tanks in history – the PzKpfw V Panther and the PzKpfw VI Tiger. Regarding the Panzer IV, this core tank went through numerous upgrades to armour and weaponry, the ultimate incarnation of the latter being the 75mm KwK 40 L/28, which was perfectly capable of disposing of a T-34. The Panther tank was even more formidable. It was designed specifically in response to meeting not only the T-34, but also the Soviet KV-1 heavy

The legendary Panther tank, here seen during Germany's ill-fated Ardennes campaign in late 1944. The major production version was the Ausf G, of which 2953 were built in the last year of the war. (Cody Images)

Did you know?

The Panther had a five-man crew, who consisted of driver, radio-operator/hull machine gunner, commander, gunner and loader.

tank, a slow-moving massively armoured monster which later, in the KV-2 variant, even had a 152mm gun and armour up to 110mm (4.33in.) thick. The Panther imitated the sloping armour, low profile and wide tracks of the T-34, and its powerful Maybach engine could push it to 46km/h (29mph). It was also armed with the long-barrelled 75mm gun, with seventy-nine rounds of ammunition carried internally.

The Panther was thrown into action, too early, in 1943 at the battle of Kursk, where mechanical problems plagued its performance. It never entirely freed itself from technical issues, but improved versions of the Panther became some of the feared armoured vehicles on all fronts, accounting for hundreds of Allied tanks.

The Panther's potential claim as the war's greatest tank had a contender in the Tiger.

The formidable Tiger tank was the last thing many Allied tank crews saw. Its combat strength lay in its 88mm gun, which could penetrate virtually all Allied armour of the time.
(Cody Images)

Did you know?
The M3 had a length of 4.45m (14ft, 10in.), weighed 14,700kg (32,413lb), had a maximum armour depth of 51mm (2in.) and could travel at a max speed of 58km/h (36mph).

The Tiger's development actually began before the war, but when it emerged on the battlefield in 1942 in North Africa there was nothing to touch it. It was a huge vehicle, weighing 55 tonnes (54 long tons) and with armour equalling the depth of that on the KV-2. Its bulk and weight made it slow, but it was armed with an 88mm gun that delivered exceptional reach and penetration. Like the Panther, it suffered from its fair share of mechanical issues during the early years of operation, but it became one of the Allies' worst nightmares, particularly with the creation of the Tiger II variant, which had thicker armour and a more potent 88mm gun. In one incident, not untypical, in Normandy in 1944 a single Tiger took out twenty-five Allied tanks before it was finally destroyed. Only limited Tiger production numbers and growing Allied air superiority controlled the Tiger's effects.

Apart from the American M26 Pershing tank introduced at the very end of the war, with its 90mm gun, and the Sherman Firefly (see below), the Western Allies made few tanks that directly matched a Panther or Tiger in terms of capabilities. British tanks such as the Covenanter, Crusader, Churchill and Cromwell were nonetheless effective when used intelligently (which they were often not), and huge numbers of American vehicles, also supplied in large numbers to British and Soviet forces through Lend-Lease (the programme under which the US supplied Britain, the Soviets, France and other Allied nations with materiel during 1941–45), helped tip the balance of armoured warfare in the Allies' favour.

◀ *The M4 Sherman tank was available in huge numbers to Allied forces, and could hold its own against a Panzer IV. One of its unfortunate design attributes was that it could be hard to escape from if hit and burning. (Cody Images)*

ETERNITY
T.

Light armour was particularly numerous in Western Allied armies. For example, the M3 Light (Stuart) Tank, served in both American and British forces – in the latter it was nicknamed the 'Honey'. Lightly protected, and armed with a 37mm gun, it was more irritating than dangerous to heavy tanks, the Stuart was soon taken out of frontline combat, but like the legions of other light vehicles and armoured cars used in the war, it proved excellent for reconnaissance and infantry support duties. Some of these vehicles did acquire firepower heavy enough to worry a medium tank – the British AEC Mk III was fitted with the same 75mm gun as mounted on many Cromwell and Churchill tanks. Other examples include the US M8 and T18E2 Boarhound, and (on the opposing side) the German SdKfz 234. Combined with fleets of scout cars with lighter armament, including the M20 Armoured Utility Car and the Daimler Scout Car, infantry were rarely far away from some form of armoured vehicular support.

The greatest of all the Allied armoured vehicles, however, was the M4 Medium (Sherman) tank. A good all-round medium tank, the basic Sherman M4A1 had a 75mm M3 gun, a maximum armour depth of 62mm (2.4in.) and a speed of 34km/h (21mph). Its profile was a bit high, and it had the unfortunate capacity to burn easily when hit by an enemy shell. But with US industrial might behind it, the Sherman was produced in decisive numbers – about 50,000 (all variants). Later versions such as the M4A3 and British Sherman Firefly were even fitted with powerful, long-barrelled 76mm guns capable of taking out a German Tiger or Panther.

▶ The Sherman Firefly was a regular Sherman fitted with a 17pdr (75mm) high-velocity gun, sufficient to destroy even a German Tiger or Panther. They were put to good use during the advance through Normandy in 1945. (Cody Images)

▶▶ A British Churchill tank grinds through the tough bocage terrain in Normandy, 1944. Despite being a large tank, it could move fast – in fact it had to be regulated to 61km/h (38mph) to stop it damaging its tracks and suspension. (Cody Images)

SPECIALIST AND UTILITY VEHICLES

Tanks such as the Sherman, T-34 and Panzer IV provided the chassis for a very large number of specialist vehicles, including assault guns, tank-destroyers, self-propelled guns, rocket launchers, mine-clearing vehicles, armoured flame-throwers and bridge-layers. The Churchill and Sherman tanks in particular were converted into some real oddities, including the Sherman DD (Duplex Drive), a Sherman tank transmuted into an amphibious vehicle via a collapsible fabric screen and two propellers mounted at the rear.

Tanks themselves required whole fleets of support machines to keep them in action, particularly in the form of recovery and engineering vehicles. The hull and chassis of the Sherman tank, for example, were used as the platform for an A-frame crane and winch with a 27,210kg (60,000lb) pull capacity, this American vehicle was known as the M32. German armoured units made a similar conversion of Panther tank to produce the Bergepanther tank recovery vehicle.

Half-tracks also came of age in World War II, and not only in the APC role that they established in the interwar period. The German SdKfz 250 and 251 platforms

An International Harvester TD-18 tractor pulls a US 155mm howitzer through the jungles of the Solomons in 1943. The terrain on most Pacific islands meant that heavy tractors such as these were in high demand. (Cody Images)

Did you know?

The Churchill ARVE (Armoured Vehicle Royal Engineers) could perform a number of pioneer duties depending on the variant, ranging from laying log roads and filling trenches with bundles of brushwood, to destroying enemy bunkers with a 290mm spigot mortar.

71

> *The Morris Quad CMP was an Allied artillery tractor, typically used to pull 17pdr or 25pdr field guns. The CMP initials stood for Canadian Military Pattern. (Cody Images)*

◀ *The German vehicle here is the eight-wheeled SdKfz 232 radio-command vehicle; the wire frame fitted over the top of the car is a long-range radio antenna. The eight-wheel configuration made these vehicles highly mobile. (Cody Images)*

were mounted with a broad variety of weapon systems, such as turret-mounted 20mm cannon (SdKfz 250/9) and 75mm Pak 40 anti-tank guns (SdKfz 251/22). For the Allies, the defining half-track was the Carrier, Personnel Half-track M3, produced in quantities approaching 43,000. With a lively cross-country capability and a top speed of 64km/h (40mph), the initial model could carry up to thirteen occupants and could be reconfigured to all sorts of useful utility and combat configurations. For instance, the M4 81mm Motor Mortar Carriage (MMC) did exactly what it stated, the rear cargo bay holding an 81mm that could be fired either mounted or dismounted. The T19 version, meanwhile, had nothing less than a 105mm M2A1 howitzer on the back, making an improvised self-propelled gun. Other versions included field ambulances and engineer vehicles.

World War II spawned a whole new generation of light, multi-purpose utility vehicles. On the Allied side, the most famous of these was undoubtedly the Willys MB Jeep, manufactured by Willys and the Ford Motor Company between 1941 and 1945. These tough, fast, four-wheel drive vehicles, with their iconic shape, were applied across numerous utility roles from serving as staff cars to handling battle casualties, and many versions were mounted with machine guns for light defence. Similar vehicles in wartime service included the Volkswagen Kübelwagen (German), Humber Heavy Utility Car (Britain), and the GAZ-67B (Soviet Union).

Light but fully tracked vehicles were also developed to carry out minor resupply

The Bren Gun Carrier was a useful British/ Commonwealth light utility and reconnaissance vehicle. Here Canadian soldiers have adapted the carrier to take a Vickers machine gun. (Cody Images)

At Salerno in Italy, a German SdKfz 10 ascends some tricky terrain. The SdKfz was a light utility vehicle and troop transporter; here we see it pulling a light anti-tank gun, while the gun crew sit in the back. (Cody Images)

These Special Air Service (SAS) troopers are driving one of the most famous light utility vehicles of the war – the Willys 'Jeep'. Here they have armed the Jeep with three Vickers K machine guns. (Cody Images)

and reconnaissance duties. The British, for example, utilized the Universal Carrier Mk I built by Vickers-Armstrong. This vehicle was powered by a 63.4kW (85hp) 8-cylinder Ford V8 engine and could carry four people (including two crew) inside a light armoured box, with defensive armament provided in the shape of a 0.303in. Bren Gun (hence the vehicle's popular name, the 'Bren Gun Carrier'), and sometimes a 14mm Boys anti-tank rifle. A similar vehicle produced by the Americans was the M28 Weasel, which was appreciated for its ability to lug cargo over almost any terrain, including snow and mud, and for its amphibious abilities – it could achieve a maximum water speed of 6km/h (4mph).

Wartime innovation proved that a core vehicle could be adapted to a multitude of applications, and the world of trucks

Yes, it's bad inside the tank but, my God, it's a damned sight worse outside.

Ken Tout, World War II veteran

was no exception. Improved techniques of industrial mass production ensured that the truck was the primary means of frontline resupply (although horses were still used in huge numbers, particularly on the Eastern Front). The Axis powers were actually the least well served in terms of truck volumes during the war: Germany produced nearly 346,000 trucks between 1939 and 1945, alongside Italy's 83,000 and Japan's 166,000. Looking at the Allies, the British manufactured a respectable 481,000 and the Soviets a weak 197,000, but both these powers were supported by the vast

◄ The Hotchkiss H35 was a light tank adopted into French service in the mid-1930s. It was a small vehicle just 4.22m (13ft 10in.) long, and despite upgrades in 1939 it performed poorly during the battle of France in 1940. (Cody Images)

◀◀ US Lend-Lease provided the Red Army with many of its trucks. Here Soviet infantry in 1945 are riding American GMC 6x6 2½-ton vehicles, powerful heavy lifters. (Cody Images)

◀ Dodge trucks fulfilled a huge variety of purposes during World War II. The WC 54 vehicle here is serving as an ambulance during the advance into Germany in 1945. (Cody Images)

Conditions on the Eastern Front put the harshest strain on trucks. Soviet trucks, such as the ones seen here, were very basic vehicles, but coped well with sub-zero temperatures. (Cody Images)

The Soviet T40A was designed as an amphibious tank, but following its poor performance in the Winter War against the Finns it was converted to land operations only. (Cody Images)

output of the United States – 2,382,000 units, with large numbers exported as part of Lend-Lease.

The US vehicles included some of the great names of automotive history: the Dodge WC series, the GMC 6x6 and the

83

formidably powerful Mack NO, a 6x6 vehicle stretching 7.5m (24ft 8in.) long and weighing in at 7.5 tonnes (7.4 long tons). The Germans also had some very fine trucks, such as the Büssing-Nag 454 and the Opel Blitz, but they simply weren't available in the massive truck fleets enjoyed by the Allies.

TAKING TO THE WATER

A distinctive innovation of the World War II years was the rise of the amphibious vehicle. The sheer diversity and extent of the war's theatres, which ultimately stretched from Scandinavia down to the South Pacific waters, meant that successfully negotiating water obstacles was essential for both overland advance and for coastal invasions. On the whole, Germany made limited investment in amphibious assault vehicles.

From 1942 it introduced small numbers of the Land-Wasser-Schlepper amphibious tractor onto the Eastern Front and North Africa, which could cross short expanses of water with twenty passengers on board while also towing a floating cargo trailer. A lighter, but more prolific, German amphibious vehicle was the Volkswagen Schwimmwagen (Types 128 and 166). This useful little vehicle was essentially a Kübelwagen fitted with a flotation body and a chain-driven propeller fitted to the rear of the 'hull'. The angle of the front wheels acted as the rudder.

For the Allies looking across oceans and seas to reclaim occupied territories, the need to develop amphibious vehicles was much more imperative. The primary duty of such craft was to transfer troops and materiel from offshore vessels to invasion

Did you know?

The DUKW performed as well on land as on water, with a range of 640km (400 miles) on a single fuel tank and a maximum road speed of 80km/h (50mph).

beaches, as quickly and securely as possible, then fight on land if necessary. In terms of wheeled vehicles, the British developed the 12-tonne (11.8-long ton) Terrapin Mk 1 as an amphibious cargo transporter, and the Americans produced the Ford General Purpose Amphibious (GPA), basically a waterborne version of the Willys Jeep. The most famous of all, however, was another American vehicle, the DUKW 'Duck'. More than 21,000 of these useful 6x6 vehicles were built by GMC from 1942. Looking distinctly more like a boat than a truck, it could carry twelve troops or 2.3 tonnes (2.26 long tons) of equipment across water at a speed of 10km/h (6mph) for a range of 93km (58 miles). The DUKW was used extensively across most Allied theatres, including the D-Day landings in Normandy on 6 June 1944.

The pressures to perfect amphibious warfare were nowhere greater than in the Pacific. US Marine and Army forces were, from 1942, fighting an 'island hopping' campaign across the planet's biggest expanse of water, putting troops and equipment onto tiny scraps of land in the face of blistering resistance and difficult coastal terrain.

The Landing Vehicle, Tracked (LVT) series of amphibious assault vehicles were an ideal solution to conducting these operations successfully. They were fully tracked craft, the tracks providing both a method of propulsion through the water and good traction on soft beaches or muddy coastal regions. The original LVT 1 was capable of carrying eighteen fully equipped soldiers or 2,041kg (4,500lb) of cargo, but its lack of armour was soon revealed as a major

A British despatch rider on a BSA motorcycle stops to talk with the crew of a Humber Light Reconnaissance Car (LRC). As its name suggests, the LRC was used by reconnaissance troops, who relied mainly on its fast 72km/h (45mph) top speed to get it out of trouble. (Cody Images)

issue on the contested Pacific beaches. Therefore subsequent LVTs in the series received increasingly heavy armour and firepower, turning them into true assault vehicles. The LVT(A), for example, was mounted with the turret from an M3 tank, complete with its 37mm gun. (More typical armament was combination of 0.3in. and 0.5in. Browning machine guns fixed into swivelling shield mounts.) Such vehicles were a critical ingredient in the success of American amphibious actions in the Pacific, and they were also used in Italy and Northern Europe in the final months of the war in those theatres.

Amphibious vehicles, as we have seen, were just one example of the impressive innovation shown by military engineers and designers during World War II. In a war defined by manoeuvre and the quest for tactical advantage, military vehicles were now the critical factor in land forces warfare. Not only were they at the vanguard of major advances, but they were also central to logistics, battlefield engineering, command-and-control (in the form of radio cars), medical evacuation, amphibious assault and numerous other duties. The war ended in Europe in May 1945, and in the Pacific the following September. The lessons learnt in World War II were taken forward into the vehicle designs of the Cold War, where they would achieve new levels of sophistication in a computerized age.

In a sense, the basic types of military vehicle changed little in the second half of the 20th century from those established during World War II. The Cold War battlefield was still a place of tanks (of various weights), armoured cars, APCs (in their broadest categories), trucks, light utility vehicles and so on. What changed dramatically was the lethal potential of even the smallest vehicles through the invention of modern anti-tank guided missiles (ATGMs), which also brought the corresponding need for advanced armour and protection systems. In turn, these developments also brought about a new military vehicle type – the infantry fighting vehicle (IFV) – a sort of midway point between the APC and what became known as the main battle tank (MBT). All these changes took place in the context of increasing computerization of war-fighting and logistical technologies, increasing the capabilities of Cold War military vehicles exponentially compared to their World War II predecessors.

Looking first at tanks, which from the 1950s had to operate in the increased threat environment presented by ATGMs, what we see is a progressive development of armour, armament, mobility and fire-control. Armour now had to cope with the shaped-charge warheads of ATGMs, as well as more effective tank shells, such as the high-explosive anti-tank (HEAT) and the later armour-piercing, fin-stabilized, discarding-sabot (APFSDS). For this reason, during the 1960s–80s, armour tended to

> Armor – The Combat Arm of Decision
>
> Motto of the US Army Armor Branch

The US M60A2 tank had a weapon that could fire both conventional shells and MGM-51 Shillelagh anti-tank guided missiles. The vehicle was not a success, however, and was withdrawn from service in the early 1980s. (Cody Images)

An Iraqi T-55 tank lies destroyed north of Kuwait City in 1991. Soviet-era Iraqi armour was completely outclassed by coalition tanks, and also fell easy prey to coalition strike aircraft. (Cody Images)

Did you know?

In the 1970s, the British introduced their Chobham multi-layered, composite armour, designed to defeat shaped-charge warheads. First fitted to the Chieftain tank, its exact composition is still a secret.

become both heavier (i.e. thicker) and more multi-layered in design to cope with more sophisticated warheads. In the 1980s explosive reactive armour (ERA) made its appearance. ERA consisted of explosive panels on the outside of the tank that detonated when struck by a shell; the outward force of the ERA blast was intended to counter the inward impact of the enemy shell or missile. The threat of nuclear, biological and chemical (NBC) warfare also meant that many tanks had to be fitted with the required survival systems for operating in radioactive or poisonous environments.

As armour became harder to puncture, so tank guns increased in their power, range and lethality (aided by the ammunition types described above). A good example of this shift can be seen in the British Centurion tank of the 1950s. Between 1945 and 1959 its main armament was progressively upgraded from 76mm to 83.8mm to 105mm. Centurions were eventually replaced in the 1970s by the Chieftain tank, which had a 120mm gun and was wrapped in the new Chobham armour. Soviet forces also upgraded their firepower. The great series of Soviet post-war MBTs – vehicles such as the T-54, T-55, T-62 and T-72 – took on heavier armament, working up from the 100mm guns of the T-54 and T-55 to the 125mm guns of the T-64, T-72 and T-80.

▲ The AMX-30 is a French MBT, but here it is seen in Saudi Arabian service. It is armed with a 105mm gun, plus a coaxial 20mm cannon, and it is protected by a full NBC suite. (Cody Images)

The M60A1 Armoured Vehicle-Launched Bridge (AVLB) is fitted with a scissors-type bridge that can be emplaced across an 18m (60ft) gap in just two minutes. Retrieval takes 10 minutes. (Cody Images)

Did you know?
Gyroscopic gun stabilization was introduced into Cold War tank gun systems. It meant that a tank gun could maintain its aim point even when the tank was moving over rough ground.

The United States moved with the trend also. In the early post-war years, and apart from small numbers of heavy tanks such as the M103 with its 120mm gun, the US Army fielded three principal medium tanks – the M46, M47 and M48 – which were armed with 90mm guns. Yet with the introduction of the M60 in 1956, the Army switched to the 105mm gun, and versions of the M48 were also upgraded to this calibre.

As MBTs were up-gunned, they were also beneficiaries of profound changes in fire-control systems. Optical range-finders were introduced on tanks such as the M47 and German Leopard 1, then in the 1960s

◀ The M1 Abrams virtually represents perfection in tank design. Its only drawback is the voracious fuel consumption from its gas turbine engine, although this same engine can push the vehicle to speeds of more than 70km/h (43.5mph). (Cody Images)

laser range-finders began to appear. A decade later, and sophisticated fire-control computers started to transform armoured warfare gunnery, automatically adjusting the aim point to compensate for factors such as wind speed, air temperature, ammunition type and even barrel condition, dramatically increasing the first-round hit probability.

Many Cold War MBTs fall into the category of 'classic' – the Soviet T-72; the British Chieftain and later Challenger; the Israeli Merkava; the French AMX-30. To illustrate how far MBT technology has come since 1945, however, the US M1 Abrams is a perfect example. Entering service in 1983, the M1 was a big vehicle of more than 57 tonnes (56 long tons), but driven by a 1,119kW (1,500hp) Lycoming gas-turbine engine it could develop a maximum speed of 67km/h (42mph). Its sophisticated

Many of our tanks were hit. We had never come up against anything like it before.

Israeli tank crewman, having encountered anti-tank missiles in the Yom Kippur War, 1973

Chobham-type armour was resistant to all but the heaviest anti-tank weapons. The initial main gun was a 105mm rifled type, but with the 1990 M1A1 variant this was upgraded to a 120mm smoothbore gun that, allied to its impressive computerized fire-control suite, could engage targets with first-round kills out to 3,000m (3,280yds). Standard equipment included a commander's independent thermal viewer, position and navigation control, internal diagnostic systems, integration into networked command-and-control and full NBC protection. Such vehicles are a long

▶ *The British Chieftain was one of the great tanks of the Cold War era, with an excellent long-range gun. Here we are looking down the business end of the 120mm L11 series rifled gun. (Cody Images)*

During counter-insurgency operations in Malaya in 1952, a British Daimler armoured car parks alongside a Dodge truck that is being used as a mobile command post. (Cody Images)

way from the welded or riveted steel machines of the World War II era.

APCS AND IFVS

The end of World War II put the final nail in the coffin of horse-drawn military logistics, and while footslogging would remain a part of infantry life to this day, the requirements of manoeuvre warfare meant that larger numbers of soldiers would be deployed to the frontlines in APCs. Crudely categorized, modern APCs fell into two types – wheeled and tracked. Tracked APCs offered superior off-road capability but lower speeds on-road, whereas the reverse was true of wheeled variants. The Cold War armies, therefore, tended have a mix of both types.

The greatest of the Cold War APCs, at least in terms of distribution and influence, has to be the US M113. Designed to be airportable, the M113 was essentially a powered metal box, the outer walls made of aluminium armour. It could carry eleven troops plus its two-man crew, was armed with a single pintle-mounted 0.5in. machine gun, and had a maximum road speed of 68km/h (42mph), and was also amphibious.

Although basic, the M113 demonstrated an incredible ability to be adapted and modified to multiple and various purposes. Just a few of its variants included mortar carriers, smoke generators, anti-aircraft vehicles (equipped with both multi-barrel cannon and surface-to-air missiles), cargo transporters, engineer and recovery vehicles and command posts. It demonstrated what would be a distinctive trend of post-war APCs – the ability to transform

Did you know?
The M113s were amongst the most mass-produced military vehicles in history. More than 80,000 of the type have gone into service to date.

their combat capability by adding the latest combat systems. All of a sudden, light armoured vehicles became a genuine threat to MBTs and supersonic jets, even as they performed traditional logistical and infantry-deployment roles. What this led to was the creation of dedicated IFVs, vehicles designed to serve like an APC but offer greater firepower in attack and support roles.

◀ Soviet-era vehicles formed the armoured contingent of many Cold War armies, particularly those in the Middle East. Here is a BMP-1 formerly in the service of the Iraqi Army. (Cody Images)

The Soviets led the way with vehicles such as the BMP-1 in the late 1960s. It was a tracked, fully amphibious vehicle capable of carrying three crew and eight additional troops, but what separated it from any of the Western vehicles around at the time was its extensive turret-mounted armament – one 73mm cannon, an externally mounted Sagger ATGW, and a 7.62mm coaxial machine gun. Here was

Did you know?

The AT-4 Sagger wire-guided anti-tank missile was used heavily by the Egyptians during the 1973 Yom Kippur War against Israel. Some sources say that 800 Israeli tanks were lost to the missile.

a light armoured vehicle that delivered as much combat force as utility.

The appearance of the BMP-1, and other similar types, prompted Western forces to develop their own ranges of IFVs, the turreted configuration offering a diverse spectrum of weapon mounts. During the 1970s, European IFVs included the German Marder and the French AMX-10P, while the United States produced the Armored

Infantry Fighting Vehicle (AIFV), which was essentially an M113 with improved armour, fully amphibious capability and a turreted 25mm Oerlikon cannon. Like many IFVs, the AIFV also had firing ports in the hull so all the soldiers carried inside could shoot outwards. The greatest of the American IFVs, however, has been the Bradley M2/M3 of the 1980s, with its advanced armour system plus one 25mm Bushmaster Chain Gun, one 7.62mm coaxial machine gun and two TOW anti-tank missile launchers. The British equivalent would be the Warrior Mechanised Combat Vehicle (MCV), produced from the mid-1980s and armed with a 30mm Rarden cannon. IFVs also come in wheeled varieties, such as the

Did you know?

The Warrior MCV has a crew of three, plus it can carry seven fully equipped soldiers. Its armour type is classified but it has full NBC protection and night-vision equipment for each of its crew members.

The Alvis Striker was a tracked anti-tank missile launcher, and part of the Scorpion family of vehicles. It was armed with ten Swingfire anti-tank guided weapons (ATGWs), fired from a five-missile launcher unit.

US Marine Corps' eight-wheeled LAV-25, which has seen service in mortar, anti-tank, air defence, recovery, command-and-control, logistics, fire-support and electronic warfare variants. As experience in war zones such as Iraq and Afghanistan has proven, IFVs can provide a dramatic firepower advantage and increase the survivability of the troops they carry inside.

It should be noted that there are several more categories of modern armoured combat vehicles other than those described above, but space does not allow for more than a brief summary. IFVs, to some extent, stole the thunder of traditional armoured cars, hence the newer Cold War generations carved their niche by offering greater levels of fire support, similar to those of medium tanks. The French Panhard ERC 90 F4 Sagiae, for example, is a six-wheeled vehicle armed with a 90mm gun with full computerized fire-control. Vehicles offering similar firepower include the Canadian Cougar Wheeled Fire Support Vehicle and the American Dragon Armored Fighting Vehicle.

Artillery was also increasingly mechanized, with numerous types of self-propelled guns on both tracked and wheeled mounts (good examples are the French GCT 155mm and the South African G6 Rhino), and also tactical missile launchers such as the formidable Vought M270 Multiple Launch Rocket System (MLRS). The latter was capable of destroying a football pitch-sized area of ground in seconds with a twelve missile barrage of submunition-loaded rockets firing to ranges of 300km (186 miles). Against aircraft threats, light armoured vehicles and also trucks were mounted with SAM systems and multi-barrel/multiple radar-controlled

◄A British FV107 Scimitar armoured vehicle conducts a patrol in Bosnia in the 1990s. The Scimitar bears a resemblance to the FV101 Scorpion Light Tank, but it is armed with a 30mm Rarden cannon instead of a 76mm gun. (Cody Images)

Did you know?

During the 1991 Gulf War, Iraqi forces struck by the MLRS found the experience of airburst shrapnel warheads so traumatic that those who survived called the system 'Black Rain'.

The SA-6 Gainful consists of three SA-6 surface–to-air missiles mounted on the modified chassis of a ZSU-23-4 air defence vehicle. The missiles can reach out to a range of 22km (13.7 miles). (Cody Images)

air-defence cannon. Battle-tested in conflicts including several Arab-Israeli wars and major Indo-Pakistan tank battles in the 1970s; all such armoured systems conspired to make the modern battlefield more lethal than ever.

LIGHT AND HEAVY LOGISTICS

Changes in the world of military utility vehicles since the end of World War II have been less visibly dramatic than those that have occurred in armoured fighting vehicles. Yet the Cold War era did introduce important transformations in capability, and also some new formats. There have also

◀ 'Jeep'-type vehicles extended their service well into the Cold War. Three US soldiers here stare from their Jeep across the Berlin Wall during the 1960s; an M60 machine gun is mounted on the back.
(Cody Images)

The legendary 'Humvee' is an extremely versatile infantry platform, capable of taking various different weapons configurations. The vehicle here has a .50-cal Browning M2HB in a dedicated weapons system on the roof. (US Army)

been some post-war vehicles justifiably described as classics. Probably the two most recognisable are the British Land Rover and American High-Mobility, Multi-Purpose Wheeled Vehicle (HMMWV), the latter commonly known as the 'Humvee'.

The Land Rover Half-Ton was, from the 1960s to the 1980s, the standard British Army light utility vehicle, derived from Land Rover's commercial Series IIA. Its four-wheel-drive configuration, and its resilience in the face of all manner of punishment, made it a popular addition to the British armed forces. The Humvee, by contrast, emerged after the military Land Rover had been in service for twenty decades. It replaced a range of existing small utility vehicles, and also became a major combat vehicle for both the US Army and the Marine Corps, with weapons mounted including Mk 19 grenade launchers, M2, M249 and M240G/B machine guns, and even TOW missile systems.

Regarding logistics, military trucks began a steady shift from simple workhorses to advanced vehicular platforms. During the 1950s, many military trucks, particularly in the Soviet Union, were war surplus stocks, but during the 1960s and '70s new designs were introduced such as the KrAZ-255B, Ural 375D (both Soviet), M813 (United States) and Land Rover One-Tonne (UK).

What was distinctive about these vehicles was that they variously incorporated design features that would later become standard fit, as armies moved away from militarized civilian trucks to purpose-built military vehicles. These features included driver-operated tyre-pressure adjustment, fully enclosed cab with NBC protection, multi-type brake systems and even amphibious capabilities (such as the American M520 Goer and the British Stalwart).

Trucks also became platforms for roles other than logistics. The redoubtable US M35 series of trucks, over its impressive

Good logistics is combat power.
Lieutenant-General William G. Pagonis

▶ The M35 series of trucks has given its logistical capabilities to the US Army from the 1950s to the present day. This specific cargo variant is the M44A2. (Cody Images)

▶▶ The huge weight of modern MBTs requires equally impressive tank transporters. The vehicle here is a Unipower 8x8 transporter, capable of pulling an entire Abrams tank on its trailer. (Cody Images)

60-year plus lifespan, variously transmuted into fuel transporters, engineering vans, wrecker and construction vehicles and even heavily armed gun trucks, acting as escorts to US convoys travelling through the Vietnamese hinterland during the Vietnam War (1963–75). In time, the militarization of trucks would lead to their being used in a broader range of combat roles, particularly as mounts for rocket-launchers, cruise missiles, SAM and tactical nuclear missile systems. Because of their increasingly combat-oriented profile, many trucks began to receive armoured cabs – the Soviet Ural 4320B cab could shrug off fire even from mighty 12.7mm (0.5in.) machine guns. Modern trucks, therefore, contribute more to the operational life of armed services than just shifting supplies from A to B.

While the largest of trucks could transport entire tanks, at the small end of the scale the post-war period also saw investment in

So-called 'KP cars' were manufactured by both Volvo and Scania, and featured an unusual tower design for the machine gunner. They were used by Swedish UN personnel in the Congo in the 1960s. *(Cody Images)*

Logistics … as vital to military success as daily food is to daily work.

Captain A.T. Mahan

numerous light utility transports designed to improve small-unit logistical capabilities. Some types bordered on the ingenious. One such example was the M561 Gama-Goat (again American), a six-wheel vehicle split into a front powered section and a coupled rear section. The flexible coupling between the two halves meant the Gama-Goat could haul itself across the most convoluted terrain, it was also amphibious. These light utility vehicles lifted the load from the soldier's backs and the flow of supplies to the frontline was much improved.

SECURITY

The Cold War was a time in which many armies, particularly those with membership of NATO, were heavily involved in peacekeeping operations, facing situations somewhere between humanitarian aid

Did you know?

Introduced in 1956, the US M274 Mechanical Mule was essentially nothing more than a chassis, an engine, and a seat and controls for one driver, yet it could usefully haul a 450kg (1000lb) load on its flatbed.

and outright combat. For this reason, the post-war period to the present day has seen the increasing use of security vehicles – essentially unarmed or lightly armed utility vehicles with armour protection from insurgent attack or riot. In the UK's long-standing deployment in Northern Ireland, the affectionately titled Humber 'Pig' was a regular feature, taking up

Did you know?

In Northern Ireland, and depending on the vehicle's configuration, a Humber 'Pig' could attract the following nicknames: Flying Pig, Holy Pig, Kremlin Pig, Squirt Pig and Foaming Pig.

to eight occupants and with duties that included riot control (in which it was fitted with window grilles, additional armour and anti-barricade equipment) and casualty evacuation. Another, heavier, option was the Alvis Saracen six-wheel APC, which for peacekeeping duties often had its machine-gun armament removed. Other popular security vehicles of note are the German Sonderwagen SWI, the British Sandringham 6 (essentially a six-wheel armour-clad Land Rover) and the American Commando Ranger. Security vehicles are still very much a part of armed forces, their relevance undiminished by the end of the Cold War in 1989.

◄ *White-painted vehicles of United Nations Interim Force in Lebanon (UNIFIL) go on patrol. The vehicle at the rear is the 6x6 Sisu XA-180, an APC with capacity for two crew and 10 passengers. (Cody Images)*

In 1991, a US-led military coalition launched Operation Desert Storm, the campaign to eject the Iraqi forces of Saddam Hussein from occupied Kuwait. The land campaign saw modern American and British armour utterly dominate the older Soviet-era armoured vehicles, although as much through superior training

▶ *This Saudi multiple-launch rocket system (MLRS), like others of its type, has devastating area-fire potential. Each missile from its launcher can dispense submunitions (cluster bombs) over dozens of square metres of land. (Cody Images)*

▶▶ *US soldiers wait to collect fuel containers air-dropped in Afghanistan. Their collection vehicles are the 6x4 M-Gator Military Utility Vehicle. (Cody Images)*

as advanced technology. The role of the tank seemed confirmed, and several new/upgraded MBTs entered the field around this time, including the M1A2 Abrams, the Challenger 2, the Chinese Type 90, the Russian T-90 and the French LeClerc, with third-generation gunnery, NBC, armour and navigation systems.

Since then, however, MBTs have acquired a significant question mark over their future, seen by some as out-of-date monsters rendered obsolete by the firepower of IFVs and issues of cost and long-haul transportation. At the time of writing, therefore, few countries in the world are investing in designing brand new tanks, although more are working on upgrading existing tanks to modern requirements.

The weight of emphasis has now shifted very much to the IFVs and other lighter, easily deployable armoured vehicles, such as the Bradley, LAV-25 and Warrior introduced in the previous chapter. Such vehicles have been improved with all manner of hi-tech equipment. Blue Force Tracking systems mounted on the dashboards, for example, show the occupants the positions of all friendly and enemy forces in the area in real time, the information beamed down from satellites and aircraft.

As we can see, military vehicles have now achieved ultimate sophistication and firepower. Yet heated and politically sensitive debates have been stirred by the experience of fighting in Iraq and Afghanistan since 2001. Light vehicles such as Humvees and 'Snatch' Land Rovers – a standard Land Rover Defender 110 fitted with an additional armour kit – have proved especially vulnerable to improvised

◀ A US Army Bradley sits under shelter and camouflage in desert conditions. The Bradley is a state-of-the-art infantry fighting vehicle (IFV) armed with a 25mm chain gun and TOW anti-tank missiles. (Cody Images)

Did you know?

In US forces, the Boomerang Mobile Shooter Detection System – which can be mounted on the corner of a Humvee or Bradley – can compute the exact position from which an enemy gunman fired a shot.

explosive devices (IEDs), which typically tear such soft-skinned vehicles apart. In response, more armies are now designing Mine Resistant Ambush Protected (MRAP) vehicles, which act in traditional APC/IFV roles but have far greater resistance to destruction from IEDs. These vehicles have resilient armour set at angles that deflect explosive force away from the vehicle, whether the explosion comes from directly underneath or from an IED set high on a telegraph pole. Anti-shred tyres also

Did you know?

Modern self-propelled guns such as the German Panzerhaubitzer 2000 can deliver Multiple Rounds Simultaneous Impact (MRSI) volleys, firing multiple shells at different trajectories within a few seconds, all the shells arriving on target at the same precise moment.

Sgt Chris Freeman ... squeezed the trigger and the SABOT round sliced into the second T-72. It exploded in a flash of fire and smoke...

Captain Jason Conroy, an Abrams tank commander in Iraq, 2003

prevent the vehicle grinding to a halt if the tyres are hit. MRAP vehicles include the BAe Caiman, the Force Protection Cougar H and HE, and the Force Protection Buffalo. It is likely that MRAP principles will filter into all manner of vehicles, from armoured cars to trucks.

Controversy over the right type of military vehicle for the battlefield has also dogged

◀ A US Stryker armoured fighting vehicle provides a powerful support vehicle for American infantry teams. The metal cage around this vehicle is designed to pre-detonate incoming shaped-charge warheads. (Cody Images)

some of the most promising types of recent times. Regarding amphibious vehicles, the US Marine Corps' Expeditionary Fighting Vehicle (EFV), previously known as the Advanced Amphibious Assault Vehicle (AAAV), represents astonishing abilities on both land and water. It is self-deploying and seagoing, and can travel across water carrying seventeen Marines at a speed of 47km/h (45mph), then drive straight onto land to deploy both the soldiers and its turret-mounted 30mm II Bushmaster cannon. It has composite armour, plus protection systems from mines and NBC conditions. Despite its qualities, however, at the time of writing its future is in question, as the US armed forces seek to rationalize its inventory based on predictions of future combat conditions.

It is difficult to say which of the very latest vehicles will become 'classics', not least because the era of the 'unmanned ground vehicle' (UGV) is very much on the horizon. These are tactical and logistical vehicles that, depending on the type, can either be driven by a remote operator or can autonomously drive themselves to a given destination, using GPS guidance, advanced sensors and massive computer power to negotiate obstacles. The US Army's Multifunction Utility/Logistics and

You can have all the armour in the world on a tank, and a tank can be blown up. And you can have an up-armoured Humvee, and it can be blown up.

Secretary of Defense Donald Rumsfeld

A USMC Amphibious Assault Vehicle (AAV) takes the plunge during amphibious operations. The fully tracked vehicle can transport up to twenty-five soldiers in its hold. (Cody Images)

Did you know?

The Mk 44 Bushmaster chain gun can fire 30mm rounds at 200rpm and at a velocity of 1080mps (3500ft/sec), to a distance (on land) of 3,000m (9,842ft).

Equipment Vehicle (MULE), for example, is an autonomous system that uses a 3D laser-radar ground mapping system to negotiate everything from trees to trenches, and even distinguishes between living and inanimate things according to their heat signatures. Powered by a hybrid electric/ diesel powerplant, with each wheel driven by separate electric hub motors, the vehicle has astonishing manoeuvrability, and can take supplies into the most dangerous areas without risking crews.

The MULE, and similar vehicles in production, are just the tip of the iceberg. It may well be that in 50 years time the great age of human-driven military vehicles will be largely behind us, at least in modern armies. Such is the irresistible nature of technological progress. The lineage of such vehicles will nonetheless stretch back to when inventors first strapped machine guns to cars, or when lozenge-shaped tanks lumbered over the battlefields of France.

◄ A vision of the future? The US Army 'The Multifunction Utility/Logistics and Equipment' (MULE) vehicle is fully robotic, and can drive itself to a given destination while autonomously negotiating obstacles. (US Army)

BIBLIOGRAPHY

Church, John, *Military Vehicles of World War 2* (Poole, New Orchard Editions, 1982)

Foss, Christopher F., *Tanks and Combat Vehicles Recognition Guide* (London, HarperCollins, 2000)

Gudmundsson, Bruce I., *On Armor* (Westport, CT, Praeger, 2004)

Jackson, Robert, *Tanks and Armored Fighting Vehicles – Visual Encyclopedia* (London, Amber Books, 2009)

McNab, Chris, *Military Vehicles* (Miami, Lewis International, 2003)

McNab, Chris, *Tools of Violence – Guns, Tanks and Dirty Bombs* (Oxford, Osprey, 2008)

Van Creveld, Martin, *Technology and War* (New York, Macmillan, 1991)

Wright, Patrick, *Tank* (London, Faber & Faber, 2000)